the *Caribbean*
a legacy of love

2008-9 NMI
MISSION EDUCATION RESOURCES

* * *

BOOKS

AFRICA
Where the Decades Still Whisper
by Robert Perry

ASIA-PACIFIC
From the Rising of the Sun
by Brent Cobb

THE CARIBBEAN
A Legacy of Love
by Keith Schwanz

EURASIA
Bountiful Blessing
by R. Franklin Cook, Gustavo Crocker, Jerald D. Johnson, and T. W. Schofield

MEXICO AND CENTRAL AMERICA
A Tapestry of Triumph
by Tim Crutcher

SOUTH AMERICA
A Harvest of Holiness
Compiled by Christian Sarmiento

* * *

ADULT MISSION EDUCATION RESOURCE BOOK

100 YEARS OF MISSIONS
Editors: Aimee Curtis and Rosanne Bolerjack

the Caribbean
a legacy of love

BY KEITH SCHWANZ

Nazarene Publishing House
Kansas City, Missouri

Copyright 2008
Nazarene Publishing House

ISBN 978-0-8341-2346-5

Printed in the United States of America

Editor: Aimee Curtis
Cover Design: Darlene Filley
Inside Design: Sharon Page

Unless otherwise indicated, all Scripture quotations are taken from the *Holy Bible, New International Version*® (NIV®). Copyright © 1973, 1978, 1984 by International Bible Society. Used by permission of Zondervan Publishing House. All rights reserved.

Dedication

I dedicate this book to career missionaries Samuel and Evelyn Ovando. Samuel and Evelyn completed their missionary work while serving in the Caribbean Region and were granted retirement status by the General Board in February 2007. Previous assignments took them to the South America and Central America and Mexico regions.

The Lord bless you and keep you; the
Lord make his face shine upon you
and be gracious to you;
the Lord turn his face toward you
and give you peace (Num. 6:24-26).

Contents

Acknowledgments		9
Introduction		11
1	Multicultural Milieu	15
2	Christ of Havana	25
3	Holy Boldness	32
4	The Light Burns Bright	41
5	Cultivating the Gifts	51
6	New Light Ministries	57
7	A Cup of Water	65
8	Inspired Sending	74
9	Praise God in the Islands	85
Afterword		87
Call to Action		89
Pronunciation Guide		91

Dr. Keith Schwanz is the assistant dean and lecturer in church music at Nazarene Theological Seminary (NTS). His responsibilities include serving as director of the NTS Center for Lifelong Learning, coordinating the chapel program, and directing the Seminary Singers. Prior to moving to Kansas, Keith served as a pastor in the Northwest.

Keith is the author of several books, including *Shouts at Sunrise: the Abduction and Rescue of Don Cox*, *Words of Life and Love: World Mission Literature Ministries*, and *Meeting Jesus*, all part of NMI book series. He served as editor of *Sainteté à l'Éternel!: chants pour le peuple de Dieu* (*Holiness Unto the Lord: Songs for the People of God*, 2005), the first French hymnal produced by the Church of the Nazarene. He has written numerous articles for *Holiness Today*, *Herald of Holiness*, *Illustrated Bible Life*, and *The Preacher's Magazine*.

Keith is married to Dr. Judi Schwanz, professor of pastoral care and counseling at Nazarene Theological Seminary. Together they have taught in pastors' retreats and conferences in Mexico, the Dominican Republic, Puerto Rico, Canada, and the United States. They live in Overland Park, Kansas, and have two adult children and three grandsons.

Acknowledgments

A book project covering an entire region requires the assistance of many people. I gratefully acknowledge the contributions of the following persons:

Leaders from the region:

Dhariana Balbuena, Jennifer Brown, Samuel Candelas, Ramón Cardona, Caleb Gálvez, Andrés Hernández, Mabel Hernandez, Gregory Isaacs, Alberto Ledesma, Jean-Robert Maître, Sadrack Nelson, Daniel Pérez, Sally Ramey, Gladybell Rivera, Garfield Spencer, Miguel Angel Yuden

Current missionaries to the region:

Monte Cyr, Bill Dawson, Bryan Heil, Linda Heil, Jim Koster, Curt Luthye, Evelyn Ovando, Samuel Ovando

Former missionaries to the region:

Amy Crofford, Dave Crofford, Greg Crofford, Howard Culbertson, Terry Ketchum, Terry Read, Ruth Saxon, Scott Stargel

Friends of the region:

W. George Adams, Christie Andrews, Paul Armstrong, Courtney Cox, Dorothy Cummings, John Cunningham, Eileen Devens, Nancy Firestone, Thea Hansen,

Linda Meyer, Alissa Monterroso, William Rice, Bryan Ruby, Karen Schwanz, "Swanee" Schwanz, Fletcher Tink

Thanks to NMI editors Wes Eby (now retired), who invited me to write this book, and Aimee Curtis, who guided the project to completion. I am especially grateful to Heather Ardrey for her research assistance.

I thank my God every time I remember you. In all my prayers for all of you, I always pray with joy because of your partnership in the gospel from the first day until now (Phil. 1:3-5).

Introduction

Antioch. If I could visit just one church described in the New Testament, I would meet the congregation in Antioch. The life of this church was so vibrant that the current vocabulary proved inadequate; they had to create a new word—Christians—to capture the essence of these dynamic disciples. I love being on the cutting edge, and the Antioch church led the way as the gospel spread from Jerusalem to Judea and Samaria to the ends of the earth (Acts 1:8).

Evangelism—The Antioch Christians effectively shared the good news of Jesus Christ. Most evangelists of the era spoke only to Jews. In Antioch they shared the gospel with Greeks also. People from many world regions heard about the Savior (Acts 11:19-21).

Discipleship—When the church leaders in Jerusalem heard about the revival in Antioch, they sent Barnabas to encourage the new believers. Barnabas saw evidence of the grace of God, and with gladness he taught them how to live in the Jesus way. As these believers sent their roots down deep, even more people came to faith in Jesus. Recognizing that he needed help, Barnabas traveled northwest from Antioch to Tarsus and invited Saul to join the pastoral team. Together, Barnabas and Saul poured themselves into this dynamic congregation (Acts 11:22-26).

Compassionate ministry—When a severe famine choked the Roman world during the reign of Claudius, the Christians in Antioch provided assistance to the believers in Judea. Their love for God caused them to love their brothers and sisters (Acts 11:27-30).

Missional—While they fasted and prayed one day, the congregation in Antioch recognized God's missionary heart. As instructed by the Holy Spirit, the disciples placed their hands on Barnabas and Saul to confirm they were called by God for missionary service. After this commissioning service, Barnabas and Saul launched the first missionary journey (Acts 13:1-3).

The Church of the Nazarene in the Caribbean

In the last several months, as I talked with people about the work of the Church of the Nazarene in the Caribbean Region, I began to see characteristics of the church in Antioch. The Caribbean exhibits influences from many world areas in language, culture, and racial representation. In the Church of the Nazarene on this region you find many exemplary Christians, those who are faithful and effective followers of Jesus. There is a strong identification with God's mission and an eagerness to get involved with the spread of the gospel.

The stories in this book represent the multitude of Nazarene ministries throughout the Caribbean. While it includes some historical material, it does not specifically provide a detailed account of the past. Nor does it describe every country in the region. Instead, this work includes selected stories of recent ministries as examples of the full range of activities of those who follow *the* Nazarene.

To set the context, Chapter 1 provides a brief survey of the history of the Caribbean. In the Church of the Nazarene, all of the countries in the Caribbean Region are organized in four fields according to the dominant language or national affiliation: Spanish, English, French, and Dutch. The remainder of the book is organized according to the outline evident in the New Testament account of the church in Antioch.

Evangelism and church planting—Chapter 2 focuses on ministry in Cuba. Chapter 3 describes evangelistic ministries in other places.

Discipleship and pastoral training—Chapter 4 features the Haiti Nazarene Bible College, while Chapter 5 explores discipleship ministries on other islands.

Compassionate ministry—Chapter 6 reports on New Light Ministries, a compassionate outreach to more than 200 children in the Dominican Republic. Chapter 7 provides a glimpse of several other holistic ministries in the region.

Missional—Chapter 8 shows how Nazarenes in the Caribbean seek to participate in the Great Commission. They have become partners in God's mission.

As exciting as it would be to go back to visit the church in Antioch, I'm more thrilled to move forward with the innovative disciples of today. Join the adventure. See what God is doing through the Church of the Nazarene in the Caribbean.

Bahamas
Cuba
Haiti
Dominican Republic
Jamaica
Puerto Rico
Virgin Islands
Belize
St. Martin
Antigua
St. Kitts-Nevis
Guadeloupe
Martinique
Dominica
Aruba
St. Lucia
St. Vincent
Barbados
Grenada
Trinidad and Tobago
Guyana
Suriname
French
Guiana

Multicultural Milieu

Some of them . . . began to speak to Greeks also (Acts 11:20a).

Leontis Augustin grew restless. It wasn't the restlessness of a nervous tic or a short attention span. Leontis had the kind of restlessness that compels a person to take a risk, to launch something new, to deliberately push life's adventure to a higher level.

You see, Leontis thrived on moving toward the horizon. He was a Haitian who lived in the Dominican Republic where he learned Spanish as his second language. After completing pastoral training at the Dominican Republic Nazarene Bible College, he moved to Suriname to begin a church with services in Haitian Creole and Spanish. God blessed his efforts with fruitful ministry, but that's when the restlessness intensified.

Leontis started thinking God wanted him to begin a mission in a place where the Church of the Nazarene had never opened a work. But where? He considered neighboring Caribbean countries, and over time his prayers began to focus on Aruba, a Dutch-governed island 15

The building that houses the
Church of the Nazarene in Aruba

miles off of the Venezuelan coast. God's confirmation soon came; he and his family were to start the Church of the Nazarene in Aruba.

When Leontis contacted regional leaders about his vision for Aruba, they told him of their support but added that the current budget did not have funds for this pioneer effort. The best they could do would be to pay the expenses to move his family from Suriname. Believing God would provide everything necessary, Leontis and his family moved to Aruba on faith. In 2000 the missionary effort of the Church of the Nazarene reached this island through the persistence of a restless man.

The establishment of the Church of the Nazarene in Aruba, the church's newest ministry in the Caribbean Region, in some ways parallels how the church began in

Cuba, the oldest ministry in the region. Both began through firm conviction, great personal sacrifice, and limited financial support.

When the Pentecostal Mission joined the Church of the Nazarene in 1915, the Pentecostal Mission's work in Cuba became the responsibility of the Nazarene General Board of Foreign Missions. Begun in 1902, this ministry in Cuba had the outward appearance of being started by accident.

A missionary party from Nashville stopped in the port of Trinidad, Cuba, on their way to Colombia. When it became evident that they could not continue on to South America because of turmoil there, the group decided to begin ministry right where they were. Challenges quickly tested the group's resolve. The leader died a short time later. Others returned home. Within a year only three people of the original party of about 10 remained in Cuba. By 1905 Leona Gardner maintained the ministry alone, something she continued to do until 1914. First the Pentecostal Mission, then the Church of the Nazarene following the merger, recognized the need to provide additional missionaries to assist Miss Gardner. Several attempts were made, but for various reasons the missionaries did not stay. In 1920 the church decided to close the work in Cuba.

Leona Gardner believed God had called her to Cuba and that she should remain in spite of the church's decision to cease operations. She supported herself by teaching and continued her missionary work for a total of 25 years in Cuba.

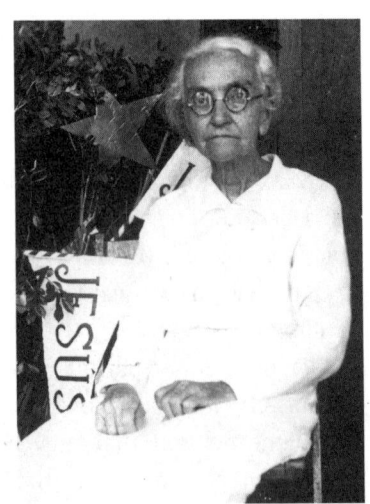

Leona Gardner

Leontis and Leona represent many national leaders and missionaries who have given their lives to build the kingdom of God in the Caribbean through the Church of the Nazarene. Some were visionaries who clearly understood God's will from the beginning. Others faithfully served as God's will became evident step by step. All sought to share the Good News, to disciple the new believers, and to graciously serve those in need.

Skirmishes and Servitude

The history of the Caribbean islands reverberates with conquest and competing claims. Christopher Columbus was the first European explorer to visit the Caribbean. He thought he had discovered a western passage to the Indies—a term that at the time referred to all of Southeast Asia, the source of exotic spices relished in European households. When the Spanish government realized the distinction, they began to refer to the islands of the Caribbean as the West Indies in contrast to Columbus's goal of reaching the East Indies.

One of the indigenous groups living in the region when Columbus arrived was the Carib people, thus the name Caribbean. The Caribbean islands divide the Caribbean Sea from the Atlantic Ocean. The Greater Antilles are the larger islands to the north: Cuba, Hispaniola (home to Haiti and the Dominican Republic), Jamaica, and Puerto Rico. The Lesser Antilles are smaller islands to the southeast: the Leeward Islands and the Windward Islands. In all, about 7,000 islands, islets, and cayes (or keys) exist in the region.

> One of the indigenous groups living in the region when Columbus arrived was the Carib people, thus the name Caribbean.

The many skirmishes to control the Caribbean had a profound impact on the cultural character development of the region. The Spaniards dominated the 16th century after Columbus claimed the entire region for Spain. Successful in its search for gold and other resources, Spain became the envy of other European countries. Thus England, France, and the Netherlands hoped to profit from their expansion and colonization in the Caribbean. Remnants of these various colonizers form an interesting blend of cultures still evident today.

Control of an island often shifted among the various

powers in the region. Sometimes a nation would gain dominance by force. Settlers from one country would try to escape to a neighboring, friendly island as the new residents waded on shore. Other times countries would buy and sell islands, seeking to improve their strategic or economic position. Occasionally people from two countries would coexist on one island. St. Martin, for example, continues to be shared by both the French and Dutch, each responsible for part of the island. Visitors hardly know when they go from one country to the other on this 33-square-mile island.

Consider, also, the varied history of St. Croix. Columbus "discovered" St. Croix on his second voyage in 1493 and claimed it for Spain. By 1625 the British held the west end of the island and the Dutch the east end. About 1645 the British routed the Dutch and controlled the whole island. In 1650 the Spanish on nearby Puerto Rico became afraid of the growing strength of the British, so they attacked and drove them out. The French recognized that the Spanish did not have strong interest in St. Croix itself, so a year later they took control. In 1733 the Danish purchased St. Croix from the French and invited settlers from any nation to move there. Since a majority of the immigrants spoke English, it became the dominant language. Fearing the possibility of an attack by way of the Caribbean during World War I, the United States purchased St. Croix from Denmark in 1917 as part of its defense strategy. St. Croix continues to be part of the U.S. Virgin Islands. Political fluctuation like this was typical for many of the Caribbean islands. Some islands experienced the change of control as many as 20 times in their history.

In addition to the skirmishes, servitude is a second mark that indelibly changed the region. The colonists soon discovered that the Caribbean is ideally suited for growing sugarcane. The explorers forced the indigenous groups into their service, but these slaves virtually disappeared because of European diseases for which they had no natural immunity. As a result the colonists began forcing Africans onto ships bound for the Caribbean. This cheap labor assured a hefty profit for the sugar plantation owners. The abolition movement, which started in the late 18th century, eventually gained momentum until the slaves were finally freed.

The loss of the slaves prompted companies to look for a new source of labor. Around 1850, indentured servants from India and China were brought to the Caribbean. In exchange for transportation to the region, housing, food, and other essentials, the indentured servants worked under contract for several years.

Eventually the governments of the Caribbean islands outlawed the oppressive practices of slavery and indentured servitude. But the mark had been made: the population of the Caribbean is racially diverse. Gradually the colonizers granted self-determination to the islands, but cultural diversity remains a distinctive feature of the Caribbean.

Caribbean Region

The makeup of the region influenced the manner in which the Church of the Nazarene structured its ministry in the Caribbean. While many regions are organized by geographical fields, the 23 countries where our church has a presence are grouped by language: Spanish, English, French, and Dutch. (See the list of the four fields and the 23 countries at the end of this book.)

Not all of the countries in the Caribbean Region are islands, however, nor are they all located in the Caribbean Sea. The Bahamas are in the Atlantic Ocean, but are usually considered part of the West Indies.

Belize, known as British Honduras until 1973, is located in Central America with Mexico at its northern border and Guatemala to the west. Since the official language of Belize is English, the only country in Central America for which Spanish is not the dominant language, Belize is part of the English Field for the Caribbean Region.

Guyana, French Guiana, and Suriname all sit on the north central border of Brazil in South America. These countries, however, have more in common with their neighbors to the north in the Caribbean than they do with the other countries in South America. Brazilians speak Portuguese; the remainder of South Americans speaks Spanish as their official language. In contrast, Guyana is an English-speaking country with half of the country of South Asian descent. Afro-Caribbean people make up 70 percent of French Guiana. Suriname sits

Pastor Carlos Moises in Aruba

between Guyana to the west and French Guiana to the east. It was a Dutch colony prior to 1975, and now Asians make up more than half of the population. The common languages and cultural backgrounds make the Caribbean Region a supportive partner for the churches in these South American countries.

When Leontis Augustin moved from Suriname to Aruba in 2000, he began holding services in Spanish and soon gathered a group of about 40 people. In many ways this endeavor reflects the diversity of the Caribbean Region. The young congregation in this Dutch country had a Haitian pastor who conducted worship services in Spanish.

The church in Aruba has continued to grow. The current pastor, Carlos Moises, is also Haitian. The congregation sings in Haitian Creole, Spanish, and Papiamento, a local language spoken only on Aruba and two neighboring islands. Pastor Moises preaches in all three languages, smoothly gliding from one to another. Some have suggested that the congregation divide into language groups, but the people strongly oppose that effort. They want to continue gathering as a truly multicultural congregation. After all, they live in the Caribbean, a multicultural milieu.

Christ of Havana

. . . telling them the good news about the Lord Jesus (Acts 11:20b).

Jeers and protests slapped the *JESUS* film team as they walked through the Santa Clara barrio. While people in that neighborhood resisted the attempt to proclaim the gospel, the courageous team members continued inviting everyone to see the film.

One man, Julio, noticed their persistence in the face of mockery. But he was most impressed with their willingness to talk with *him.* Other people in the barrio avoided him if they could. Julio accepted the invitation and went with the team members to the place where the film would be shown.

Others followed, too, including some of the cynics. Finally, impatient with the constant harassment, Julio demanded the crowd cease its complaining. "Everyone, sit down and be quiet," he commanded. They did as they were told.

People in Santa Clara had a descriptive name for Julio: "The Charro in the Black Hat." He had a violent streak and would not hesitate to attack anyone who crossed him. When his wife died after a tractor accident, he warned the coroner not to do an autopsy or he, too, would face the knife. The whisper on the street was that Julio had assassinated an adversary. The police knew Julio well, often arresting him and hauling him off to jail.

One day, in despair, Julio took a bottle of rum and a rope to a place where he could kill himself. He'd drink himself drunk, then tie his misery to the end of a rope. But he couldn't do it. Suicide was a cowardly act, he decided, and he abandoned his plan.

Soon afterward Julio met the *JESUS* film team. As he watched the film he realized Jesus was the only one who could change his life. When given the opportunity at the close of the film, Julio was one of the first to respond to the invitation. God changed the thug from the inside out.

Many others made a decision to follow Jesus that night. The *JESUS* film team members discipled the new believers until they began to function as the Body of Christ. A Nazarene congregation now ministers in that neighborhood with Julio as their pastor. The dramatic change visible in this man points to the transforming power of the gospel.

The Cuba District

"To see the lost as God sees them." This motto guides the Cuba District as they share the good news of salvation and liberation. Courageous and persistent, these entrepreneurs find creative ways to do the work of evangelism.

The Church of the Nazarene has one district for the entire country. Located about 90 miles south of Florida, Cuba's north to south dimension ranges from 22 to 160 miles; 50 miles is average. Going from east to west, the island measures 750 miles. Cuba is the largest of the Caribbean islands.

Because of transportation issues on such a large island, the Church has decentralized the responsibilities for evangelism and church planting. There are 17 evangelism coordinators to guide and encourage local efforts. They plan evangelistic endeavors twice each year. In the spring they have a local day of evangelism where each congregation determines an effective means of sharing the gospel. Each fall there is a national day of evangelism where each congregation follows the district plan.

Cuban Nazarenes have found the *JESUS* film to be an effective means of telling others about the Savior. There are four film teams in the country, each committed to planting two congregations every year. Since showings in a park or other public venues are rarely possible, most of the time a *JESUS* film team will seek permission from a family to use their house. Once arrangements are set, the team canvasses the surrounding area with invitations to the showing. Team members urge those who respond to the invitation to begin meeting for Bible study and discipleship training. They equip congregational leaders, including helping those called to pastoral ministry to begin theological education. Soon a fully functioning congregation with its own pastor exists where none had been before.

> When the last Nazarene missionaries departed Cuba in the early 1960s, they left 17 congregations and about 1,700 members.

While all Christians are to be prepared to talk about the hope they have in Christ (1 Pet. 3:15), some have been especially gifted by the Holy Spirit to do the work of the evangelist. Idalmis Fernandez is that type of woman. She is the "missionary" of the Holguín province, the second most populous province in Cuba. The Church of the Nazarene has 23 house churches in Holguín, and Idalmis started almost all of them. In one six-year stretch she planted six new congregations. Even though she has had to scale back because of illness, Idalmis continues to host mission services in her own home.

House Churches

When the last Nazarene missionaries departed Cuba in the early 1960s, they left 17 congregations and about 1,700 members. In the past several years the Church of the Nazarene has been able to open extensions of these existing congregations. Of necessity, these new works meet in homes. When a house church reaches 25 members, the district registers the congregation with the government. In 2006 the Cuba District reported 5,364 members, including 550 new Nazarenes that year.

Cuban families know the joy of hospitality. Some willingly allow more than 100 people to regularly gather at their houses for church activities. Often a person who attends a *JESUS* film showing in one house will invite the team to show the film in his or her house at a later date. This type of networking results in the planting of new churches.

The pastor in one neighborhood faced discouragement because of the difficulty in ministering in his particular area. Other Christian congregations had abandoned the place.

The *JESUS* film team prayerfully decided to go to his neighborhood. On the day of the showing, the pastor entered the area first to ascertain whether the team could safely come in. Some people had warned that the local gang would throw rocks at them if they tried to show the film. Curious about a conversation he overheard, however, the gang leader came to investigate. He was intrigued by the prospect of a film being shown in his neighborhood and pledged that nothing bad would happen to the team members.

One hundred five people viewed the film that evening, December 26, 2004. Thirty decided to follow Jesus. The gang leader offered his home so people could meet for Bible study. By 2008 the district leaders expect this group will be registered with the government as a house church. The work of courageous people leads to eternal results, even in difficult neighborhoods.

Baptismal Services

Baptism is one of two sacraments practiced by the Church of the Nazarene, and it is loaded with symbolism. The person immersed in baptism is symbolically buried with Christ and raised to new life (Rom. 6:4). Thus, baptism is a testimony that the person is a new creation in Christ—the old has gone and the new has come (2 Cor. 5:17). As a rite of initiation, baptism signifies the person has been transformed by the power of God and now identifies with the Body of Christ, the Church.

The Church of the Nazarene in Cuba perceives baptismal services not only as an act of initiation and testimony, but also as a form of evangelism. Gathering at a river or on a beach often opens opportunities for evangelistic conversations with curious bystanders.

Not long ago six congregations in the Holguín province met at a riverbank for a baptismal service, each bringing candidates with them. In the time of worship, each candidate testified to God's saving work in his or her life. Then each was baptized in the river. As the individuals emerged from the water, the gathered congregation rejoiced in God's grace and love. Curious onlookers ventured close enough to ask questions. These people may have been extremely hesitant to attend a regular church service, but they were comfortable with those worshiping God at the river. Three bystanders accepted Jesus as their Savior that day and asked to be baptized.

Similarly, four congregations from the Havana area

gathered on Guanabo Beach for a baptismal service. The crowd that gathered to observe not only listened to vibrant testimonies, they also heard a clear presentation of the gospel in a dynamic sermon. Two couples and three men accepted Jesus that day. These were fervent decisions; that evening all seven people traveled a considerable distance to attend a service at the Ceiba church. These new Christians continue to serve the Lord as part of a congregation near their homes.

On Christmas Day, 1958, Cuba dedicated Cristo de la Habana (Christ of Havana), a large statue of Christ by Cuban sculptor Gilma Madera. Sixty-five feet tall on a 10-foot base, the statue faces Havana from across the bay. It portrays Jesus with His right arm raised in an act of blessing. For the last 50 years this statue has stood as a reminder that God, through Jesus Christ, is the source of salvation and blessing. One of the ways God's blessing has been mediated is through the faithful, courageous ministry of Cuban Nazarenes. Thanks be to God!

Holy Boldness

. . . a great number of people were brought to the Lord (Acts 11:24b).

People began gathering for the parade, coming from many different directions until nearly 2,000 stood ready to step out. Those who carried musical instruments—trumpets, trombones, saxophones, and drums—created a cacophony of sound as they warmed up. Each of the 18 choirs present called its singers together, waiting for the signal to start the celebration.

With great fanfare, these Christians from the Haiti Southeast District Church of the Nazarene started the four-mile walk to the place where a baptismal service would be held. The sounds of instruments and shouts of joy filled the air as the people gave praise to God. One hundred seven persons who found the Savior through the *JESUS* film were baptized that day. One new congregation, which formed as the direct result of the work of a film team, even asked if it could be named the *JESUS* Film Church of the Nazarene.

Pastor Toto

During a time of extreme economic hardship in Haiti, church leaders called a meeting of pastors to discuss the problems faced by the churches. Some of the 60 pastors complained about their difficult circumstances. They talked of the need for a living wage and adequate housing for their families. They asked for help with transportation so they could travel to new preaching points.

The church leaders responded with words of encouragement. They urged the pastors to trust in the Lord. They advised them to teach and preach on stewardship. The more they talked, however, the more hollow their words sounded.

Then Pastor Toto stood and walked to the front of the group of pastors. His colleagues knew him as one with great experience. He began pastoral ministry when the pioneer missionary Paul Orjala served in Haiti in the 1950s. In more than 40 years of faithful ministry Pastor Toto had planted and nurtured five congregations.

The process for starting a new church remained consistent for Pastor Toto. He would move to a community, find a home, then begin a Bible study. As soon as possible they would build a brush-arbor church: dirt floor, woven banana leaf walls, and a palm branch thatched roof. Rough hewn wooden benches and an altar furnished the simple sanctuary. More than once a Work and Witness team showed up to construct a church building *after* Pastor Toto moved on to start a new congregation. As a pastor he had never known anything but the most rustic worship space.

Pastor Toto turned to look at his peers, then began to chide his fellow pastors.

"These things are not eternal," he reminded them. He opened his Bible to 2 Corinthians 4 and began to preach. "Too many of us read only the first part of the phrases: 'We are hard pressed . . . perplexed . . . persecuted . . . struck down.' That's all true, but don't forget to read the whole verse: 'We are hard pressed on every side, but not crushed; perplexed, but not in despair; persecuted, but not abandoned; struck down, but not destroyed'" (2 Cor. 4:8-9).

After a brief pause, Pastor Toto concluded, "God himself is our glory. We may not have the riches of the world, but we have the Creator of all good things as our source of strength and hope." He then returned to his seat as a spirit of optimism brightened the room.

A Work and Witness team finally caught up with Pastor Toto while he still served his fifth congregation. For the first time in his ministry the congregation had a concrete floor, concrete block walls, a tin roof, a finished altar, and sanded pews. A short time after moving into the new building, however, Pastor Toto told the district superintendent that he had identified a neighboring village where he wanted to start a new congregation, his sixth church plant. Thirty people attended the first service. Six responded to the invitation and knelt at a makeshift altar on hard-packed dirt.

Like Pastor Toto, Haitian Nazarenes plant churches

Paul Orjala

wherever they go. Haitians introduced the Church of the Nazarene in the Bahamas and Aruba. They have also planted strong churches in the Dominican Republic, Guadeloupe, and Suriname. Haitians started the Marigot church on St. Martin. In 2006 they reported 336 members and a 233 percent growth over the previous 10 years. The Haitian-led Cayenne Church of the Nazarene in French Guiana reported 385 members in 2006 and an average of 578 in Sunday morning worship.

Missionary Paul Orjala talked about the "holy boldness" of the Haitian believers. What was true in the mid-20th century remains just as descriptive at the beginning of the 21st century.

Ministry to Hindus

Large communities of Hindu people live in Suriname, Guyana, and Trinidad. For those living in the Caribbean, Hinduism provides a cultural connection with the homeland, India, from which their ancestors immigrated. A child born to a Hindu family is expected to continue in the traditional religion. As a result, Hindus tend to strongly resist the gospel.

Hindus worship 330 million gods.

The caste system, a part of Hinduism, forms a type of social security. When a person becomes a Christian, he or she threatens the social cohesion. Some new Christians are excommunicated from their Hindu families, especially in communities with strong religious adherence. Others threaten to disown the family member, then relent when the Christian stands firm.

Superstitions control many Hindus. If they are ill, they will ask a pundit to perform healing incantations. If they have perplexing questions, they may go to a Hindu fortune teller. She will drink a tea made of marijuana, work herself into a trance, then respond to questions people ask.

Hindus worship 330 million gods. Kennet, a young teenager from a Hindu family in Suriname, had a dream in which Jesus told him to attend a *JESUS* film showing. He did so without his parents' knowledge. After he made a decision for Christ, Kennet said he had been looking for one god for which to live. "I can't please all of my parents' gods," he said.

Ministry among Hindus requires a long-term commitment. The Christian must be involved in the life of the Hindu friend. Ruth Saxon, retired missionary to Trinidad, attended Hindu weddings and funerals, not as a participant in the rituals, but as a friend. The Nazarene congregation Ruth pastored in Chanka Trace was located on what people called Temple Street since Hindu temples stood at both ends. To reach Hindus it is necessary to live among them.

Hindu people in the Caribbean may regularly attend Nazarene services without making a commitment to Christ. Drawn by the Holy Spirit, they just want to be with the Christians. Disparaging comments about Hinduism would drive them away, so wise preachers take great care in what they say.

Awareness of the food habits of Hindus allows for increased opportunity for ministry. Eating together is an important function for Hindu people. Ruth tells of a fellowship time following a Sunday evening service when a Hindu girl asked if there was anything "live" in the muffins. Ruth understood the girl wondered if eggs had been used, something that would be in violation of accepted Hindu practice. Ruth assured her the muffins had been made without eggs, and the girl participated freely in the fellowship time with the Christians.

Acceptance of Christians in a Hindu community often rests on the faithful witness of those first to believe in Jesus. That was the case with Robby. His family threatened to disown him when he declared himself a Christian. When his parents would not allow him to attend church services, a Christian cousin started coming to Robby's home to pray with him. Robby's parents listened in on the prayer meetings and approved of what they heard. Eventually they allowed Robby to attend church services again. The clear testimony of grace and peace changed the minds of Robby's parents.

Few mission organizations work among the Hindu people in Guyana, making it the least-evangelized Hindu community in the world. The Church of the Nazarene has used the *JESUS* film to share the gospel with Hindus in this country. Likewise, in Suriname, the *JESUS* film has been used extensively. Teams in Suriname have shown the film in Dutch, English, Haitian Creole, French, Hindi, and Taki-Taki, a local language. The Church of the Nazarene is constantly expanding its effort to reach Hindus in the Caribbean with the hope of the gospel.

75 Years of Evangelistic Ministry in Jamaica

Charlotte Bowen slipped out of the house and made her way to the open-air meeting. When her mother discovered what Charlotte had done, she threatened to beat her daughter and lock her in the house to prevent her from attending another service. Charlotte's mother announced her intention to confront the woman evangelist too. Charlotte responded to the outburst by confidently testifying to what God had done within her that evening. Her mother's tone softened, and she never carried out any of her threats.

Once she decided to follow Jesus, Charlotte immediately began to do the work of a minister. Just 14 years old, Charlotte started visiting families living in the hills near her home. She would share verses of Scripture she had memorized and pray with the people. Charlotte preached in her first open-air meeting just a few months later. Three people accepted the Lord that night.

Many people confirmed God had gifted Charlotte for ministry. She attended Bible school as a young adult, then began doing the work of a missionary in her home country of Jamaica. Over the years she held evangelistic meetings, planted churches, strengthened young congregations, and discipled young men and women.

Known for her strong work ethic, Charlotte did not shy away from challenges. As a woman of prayer, she would rise early to talk with God. She always prayed with any person who came to her for counsel. After she left one congregation, the pastor who followed her wrote, "The fruit you left behind is just now ripening, and I am pleased to see the harvest." That was typical of Charlotte's ministry.

Not only did Charlotte do the work of an evangelist, she also poured herself into the discipleship process. She met with individuals and encouraged them to grow in the grace of God. Sometimes she spoke words of comfort, other times words of correction, but always words of hope and love.

Charlotte played an extremely important role in the lives of Garfield and Richard who grew up in the rural community of Porus. Their mother always took her children—five boys and one girl—to church. Sunday evenings were lively services at the Red Berry Church of the Nazarene with energetic, joyful singing. When Pastor Charlotte preached, everybody listened. No one was allowed to walk in and out of the sanctuary during the sermon. She permitted no talking either, and the service always concluded with an altar call.

Garfield and Richard were just 11 and 10 years old when their father died in a tragic accident. Pastor Charlotte heeded the Old Testament prophets' words to defend the fatherless. She helped the boys become established and grounded in the faith. She challenged them to high moral living through their adolescent years. When Charlotte would leave Red Berry for occasional ministries in other locations, she expected the local leaders to carry on the usual work of the church. This on-the-job training continues to bear fruit. Garfield is the pastor of the Antioch and Mandeville Churches of the Nazarene on the Jamaica West District. Richard is the pastor of the Norway Church of the Nazarene on the same district.

Charlotte Bowen began ministry as a 14-year-old girl. She faithfully served God as a minister of the gospel for 75 years. Her legacy continues through people like Garfield and Richard.

The Light Burns Bright

Barnabas and Saul . . . taught great numbers of people (Acts 11:26a).

In 2005 about 70 percent of the members of the Church of the Nazarene in the Caribbean Region lived in one country—Haiti. Currently membership stands at over 90,000 on 11 districts. There are more Nazarenes in Haiti than any other country except the United States. To understand the source of this tremendous growth we must go back to the beginning and to pioneer missionaries Paul and Mary Orjala.

Haiti occupies the western third of Hispaniola, a Caribbean island visited by Christopher Columbus in 1492. At first the whole island was governed by Spain, but eventually Spain transferred control of the western portion to France. A slave revolt against the French in 1804 resulted in Haiti becoming the first republic governed by black people.

Today Haiti is densely populated with 307 persons per square kilometer, compared with 31 persons in the United States and 3.2 persons in Canada. Haiti is the poorest country in the Western Hemisphere with unem-

Haiti is the poorest country in the Western Hemisphere. ployment rates often in the 50 to 70 percent range. The average daily income for an individual is a little more than a dollar a day (U.S.). In contrast, a minimum wage worker in the United States will earn a dollar in about 10 minutes.

The Orjalas moved to Haiti in 1950 following Paul's graduation from Nazarene Theological Seminary in Kansas City. Paul excelled as a linguist and became an authority on Haitian Creole, a hybrid language based on French used by 90 percent of the population. This language skill endeared him to the Haitian people and helped him quickly understand and adapt to the Haitian culture. As soon as he had a grasp of the language, Paul started preaching and teaching.

Equipping National Leaders

Paul believed intently that national leadership should be empowered as soon as possible. Growth would naturally follow the multiplication of leaders, he reasoned. His first priority, after gaining proficiency in Creole, was the training of pastors. Paul started what eventually became known as the Nazarene Bible Institute. Seven students formed the first class on Wednesday, October 3, 1951. This first cohort met from four o'clock to six o'clock each afternoon, three days a week.

By 1956 additional missionaries had joined the effort in Haiti, and they began construction of a campus for the Institute. At the time the selected location was 10 miles northeast of Port-au-Prince, and some questioned the wisdom of building so far out of town. In subsequent decades, however, the city has crept closer to the campus. The foresight of Paul Orjala is now remembered with gratitude. The current campus has classrooms, offices, a chapel, a library, dormitories, a cafeteria, national offices, a clinic, missionary houses, and a 1,500-seat tabernacle.

The Nazarene Bible Institute awarded its first degrees at a graduation ceremony in 1960—the year the first Haitians were ordained. At the same time, the Haitian District reported a 68 percent growth in membership. That was just the beginning of a tremendous decade for the Church of the Nazarene in Haiti. In the 1960s the number of churches increased from 119 to 405, a 340 percent increase in 10 years. The number of Nazarene members in Haiti leapt from 6,153 to 20,405, a 332 percent decadal growth.

This explosive growth came because Paul Orjala insisted on equipping and empowering national leaders. In turn, each pastor was to train other pastors. The missionaries urged the ministers to always be looking for potential preaching points in communities without a church. An existing congregation might have from one to a dozen new works in development at any moment. The pastors of these new congregations often came from within the mother church, so the early Haitian pastors not only oversaw the planting of new churches but also the training of new pastors. This approach multiplied the

Jeanine van Beek, director of Haiti Nazarene Bible College in the 1970s and 1980s

effectiveness of the church and by 1985 there were more than 47,000 Nazarenes in Haiti. The momentum has carried forward as the DNA of an evangelistic church was imprinted on the Haitian Nazarenes by an insightful pioneer missionary.

Haiti Nazarene Bible College

The trajectory of the growth line, however, has not been straight to the top right side of the graph. The process of training pastors needed reorganization in the 1970s. Jeanine van Beek reopened the Nazarene Bible Institute in 1975 after it was closed for three years. She came to Haiti from European Nazarene College (EuNC) in Switzerland where she served as academic dean from 1966 to 1975. (Jeanine later served as rector of EuNC from 1990 to 1998.)

Jeanine's availability to the students proved to be a major element in the integrative, holistic preparation of pastors. Jeanine often took a walk in the evenings, a clear indication of her availability for informal conversations with students who lived on campus. Many important issues were explored in those chats. On weekends Jeanine accompanied students for ministry in churches throughout the country. Enrollment at the Institute gradually increased from nine students in 1975, to 22 in 1980, and 50 in 1985.

Jeanine also guided the school in taking significant steps to increase the academic stature of the institution. She initiated the bachelor of theology degree, a tremendous advance in theological education in Haiti. Nazarene Bible Institute was renamed Haiti Nazarene Bible College (HNBC) and now offers a diploma in theology requiring three years of residential study. The bachelor of theology degree requires two years of study on the main campus beyond the diploma. A certificate in pastoral studies is also available.

The Haitian government recognizes HNBC as only one of a half-dozen schools approved to award the bachelor of theology degree. What was started by Paul Orjala and re-energized by Jeanine van Beek continues to serve the Church of the Nazarene well.

Jeanine van Beek Women's Dormitory

In the past few years there has been a growing openness to women pastors in Haiti. An increased number of women applicants to HNBC accompanied this trend. While the diploma and bachelor's programs required attending classes on campus, women students commuted since the dormitories were for men only. That changed in 2005 with the opening of the Jeanine van Beek women's dorm. This facility can accommodate up to eight female students.

Louis Marie Lourde, or Mary-English as she is called, became the first student resident. Nine years after she accepted Jesus as her Savior, Mary-English felt God calling her to pastoral ministry. When she began to serve as a pastor in the area of Haiti where she grew up, her obvious gifts for ministry quieted those who hassled her for being a woman in ministry. After several years of pastoral ministry, Mary-English enrolled at HNBC for additional training.

Ruth Destinè became a Christian when she was 20 years old. Consequently, her family shunned her when she left the Catholic Church. Confirmation of God's call to ministry came, however, with Ruth's increasing involvement in ministry—both as a Sunday School teacher and one who visited the sick in hospitals and in homes. Ruth now studies at HNBC and lives in the van Beek dorm. She intends to serve in pastoral ministry following graduation.

Andrèenne Pavilus made a decision to follow Jesus

at an evangelistic meeting when she was 21 years old. Her pastor recognized her gifts for ministry and encouraged her to begin theological education at HNBC. Andrèenne already dreams of doctoral studies. She now lives in the Jeanine van Beek dorm as she prepares for a preaching and teaching ministry, continuing the legacy of the woman after whom her residence is named.

The presence of women students on the Bible College campus has had a positive impact on the learning environment. At commencement in May 2006, the valedictorian said, "A seminary without women students is like a Christian without a songbook." Knowing the importance of congregational singing for Haitian Christians indicates the strong support the men students have for their women colleagues.

Passing the Torch

Sadrack Nelson often got in trouble or was injured while his mother attended church services on Tuesday evenings. The neighborhood in which they lived, one of the poorer areas of Port-au-Prince, provided enticements that could create problems for almost any 15-year-old boy. Sadrack had never met his father, so his mother had sole responsibility for him. Finally she decided it was best for Sadrack to go to church with her at the Bel Air Church of the Nazarene. She was right. During those Tuesday evening meetings Sadrack became spiritually established.

Sadrack's mother also had a profound influence on

her son's spiritual growth. What she testified to at church she lived at home. Every morning and evening she gathered her children for family devotions, Bible reading and prayer. Sadrack acknowledges that his mother influenced him greatly, especially in his spiritual formation.

When Sadrack was 18 years old, missionary Terry Ketchum held a mission conference at the Bel Air church. In that service Terry made a statement about how God often calls people to full-time ministry while they are young. Sadrack remembered as a third grader feeling God calling him to become a pastor. At that time his family wanted him to be a doctor, but Sadrack was sure God had different plans. Now many years later, God confirmed the call Sadrack first heard as a child.

When Sadrack finished secondary school, he enrolled in Haiti Nazarene Bible College. He received the diploma in theology in 1999. He continued his studies and completed the bachelor of theology degree in 2005. He is currently working on a master's degree in pastoral studies at Northwest Nazarene University.

After receiving the diploma, Sadrack became an associate pastor in his home church, Bel Air. He then became pastor of a congregation of 500, the Cité Soleil church in Port-au-Prince. This church is in a neighborhood that has spawned much of the gang violence that has disrupted life in Haiti over the past few years. Once an armed gang interrupted a worship service and demanded money. Because of the violence, people moved out of the neighborhood and attendance dropped. Church leaders warned Sadrack that it was no longer safe

Sadrack Nelson, director of theological education by extension in Haiti

for him to come into the community. He responded by starting a second congregation nearby.

Church leaders continue to watch Sadrack persist in the face of danger. He is optimistic and disciplined, a deep thinker, a man of integrity. Sadrack has a diplomatic spirit and is able to help a group find consensus. He is faithful with little, so his sphere of influence has opened wider.

Sadrack also serves God in other ways. The Haiti Bible Society began an ambitious project to print a Creole Study Bible. The Creole Bible translation was completed in 1986, and they remain on target to complete the study Bible by 2010, the first of its kind in Creole. Sadrack serves as one of five writers for this project.

Because it is economically unfeasible for many people to leave their families for three to five years of study on campus, the church has developed a theological education by extension program. Sadrack serves as the extension director in Haiti. In 2006 there were nine centers on 8 districts. The goal is to have at least one pastoral training center on each of the 11 districts. One hundred sixty-eight students enrolled in the nine centers in 2006. Besides administering the program, Sadrack developed 15 of the eventual 36 courses in the program.

Sadrack grew up in a Nazarene congregation. He trained at Nazarene schools. Now he teaches others as he has been taught, generously sharing the blessing he has received.

The Bible College in Haiti has a traditional ceremony observed at every graduation. Each member of the graduating class holds a candle. One by one, the glow moves down the line as each graduate lights the candle of the next person. When the light comes to the president of the graduating class, that person lights the candle held by the president of the next year's class. This ceremony symbolically passes the responsibility to hold high the Light of the World.

The torch continues to be passed to the next generation in Haiti. What Paul Orjala started in 1950 has reached Sadrack Nelson in 2008. Sadrack continues the process of passing the light of Christ on to those who need the Savior. The Light burns bright in Haiti.

Cultivating the Gifts

The disciples were called Christians . . . (Acts 11:26b).

The Bible calls the church to make disciples (Matt. 28:19). That process begins with evangelism and continues as believers grow in the knowledge of the Christian faith (2 Pet. 3:18). Sometimes this growth in grace occurs through formal education. Other times the faithful witness of a pastor helps a person become spiritually established and effective in ministry.

Haiti Nazarene Bible College is one of four ministerial training schools in the Caribbean Region. The others include Cuba Nazarene Bible College, Caribbean Nazarene College, and the Dominican Republic Nazarene Bible College. These four schools reported 225 residential and 731 extension students in 2005.

Cuba Nazarene Bible College offers a bachelor of theology degree and a master of arts in religion degree. Students may study Christian education as a concentration, and pastoral training is available at extension centers as well. Work and Witness teams from Canada—in addition to the construction of several church buildings—have made a tremendous contribution to the campus. A new dining hall was dedicated in January 2003. Since the campus is also used for camps, retreats, and meetings, such as district assemblies, people often fill the dining hall with conversation and laughter.

Missionaries founded the Nazarene Training College (NTC) in Trinidad on January 3, 1951. The 35-acre campus has served the school since its establishment. An accreditation team commented during a recent visit that the campus was the best of all the theological schools in the Caribbean.

NTC was created specifically to train pastors from Trinidad, but the first student to enroll came from Guyana. In the early years students from Barbados also came to the college to prepare for pastoral ministry. The region served has expanded as the church has grown in the Caribbean. Now 12 districts from the English field support the school with students and contributions. An increasing number of faculty and administrators come from the region.

The name of the school changed to Caribbean Nazarene Theological College in 1974, then to Caribbean Nazarene College (CNC) in 2005. This action reflects the expanding educational program of CNC. The school now offers a bachelor's degree in theology, Christian education, or general studies, and one master's degree in counseling. CNC has been fully accredited by the Caribbean Evangelical Theological Association since 1996.

Everyone needs to be nurtured in the faith, not only those who attend a Bible college. Perhaps the most frequent example of discipleship happens when a mature

Christian invites another person to follow his or her example. This type of discipling occurs often throughout the Caribbean Region.

Soft Spoken Mentor

When Hurricane George roared through the Caribbean in September of 1998, more than 100,000 people were left homeless in the Dominican Republic. George extensively damaged the aqueduct that provided water to Pueblo Viejo, a community of more than 5,000 in the southwest part of the country. Damage to the infrastructure adversely affected the quality of the water, and tests showed it was not safe to drink. As a result, tanker trucks began hauling water to the residents.

Leaders of the Church of the Nazarene discussed this grave need in their community. They decided to drill a well on the church's property. First one pump, then three brought potable water to the surface. At no charge to the residents, the church continues to provide the primary source of water for the people of Pueblo Viejo.

The generosity of the congregation reflects the character of their pastor. When Pastor Luis Daniel Perez sees a need, he quietly finds a way to meet it. He is not a political leader, but many in the community seek him out for solutions to problems they face. He and his wife made room in their small house for children in need of a family. They have welcomed two nephews and four nieces into their home. Luis Daniel holds great respect in the hearts of his neighbors in Pueblo Viejo.

Luis Daniel Perez, pastor and district superintendent in the Dominican Republic

Luis Daniel became a copastor of the Church of the Nazarene in Pueblo Viejo in 1984. Four years later he was named the pastor of this congregation. He completed his ministerial training in 1990 when he graduated from the Dominican Republic Nazarene Bible College. In the early years of his ministry at Pueblo Viejo, only about five people attended worship services—including Luis Daniel and his wife. In the succeeding years many others have come to faith in Jesus as this faithful man has done the work of an evangelist. Those same people then grew in the grace of God as Luis Daniel served them as an encourager.

The Pueblo Viejo church owned several musical instruments, but no one who knew how to play them. Luis Daniel recognized this as an opportunity to equip members of his church for ministry. After he identified several with musical aptitude, he found a musician in a nearby church of another denomination who agreed to provide music lessons. They began holding a music school at the church every Saturday. Luis Daniel joined the others for the music lessons because he wanted his people to see him as a learner too. By his own admission he is not as skilled as others, but if no one else is available he can play the piano for a worship service.

With the intent of showing that he is not indispensable, Luis Daniel trains members of his congregation to do the work of ministry. Every Tuesday evening they gather for instruction on how to lead a church. They learn spiritual disciplines like prayer and biblical mandates like evangelism. Luis Daniel shares from his own experience as he equips his people with skills for pastoral visitation and leadership.

> With the intent of showing that he is not indispensable, Luis Daniel trains members of his congregation to do the work of ministry.

Some who complete the training available at the Pueblo Viejo church continue their studies through the extension program of the Bible college. As a further encouragement to those called and gifted for ministry, the congregation pays the educational expenses of three students.

When the Central District divided to form the South District in September 2000, the assembly chose Luis Daniel as the superintendent of the new district. Luis Daniel was the natural choice for this office since more than a dozen women and men have gone from leadership positions in the Pueblo Viejo congregation to pastorates throughout the Dominican Republic. The cultivation Luis Daniel provided at the Tuesday evening meetings continues to bear fruit throughout the country.

As is true for approximately 85 percent of Nazarene

pastors on the Caribbean Region, Luis Daniel has another job. He has owned a plot of land since he was a young man. He grows bananas and other farm products to support his family and provide resources to fund his generosity. His most effective cultivation, however, turns the soil of a person's heart to receive the Word, then cares for the tender plant until it, too, bears fruit. And the angels rejoice at the effective ministry of a quiet pastor in the Dominican Republic.

New Light Ministries

The disciples . . . decided to provide help (Acts 11:29).

When Randy registered as a student in the New Light Ministries program at the Quisqueya Church of the Nazarene in Santo Domingo, Dominican Republic, he and his mother didn't attempt to conceal their family's dysfunction. Randy's father drank heavily. Since his dad used most of his earnings to buy alcohol, and Randy's mother didn't work outside of the home, the family often suffered without the basic necessities of life. Randy's father also beat his wife and children. The fear and intimidation from this physical abuse only intensified the emotional turmoil the family endured.

Hearing this story, and others like it, broke the hearts of the people of the Quisqueya church. It also confirmed their decision to share Jesus' love with the children in their neighborhood and strengthened their resolve to work through any and all obstacles they faced along the way.

Randy made a decision for Christ after watching the *JESUS* film for children in June 2005. With a child's faith he believed in Jesus as his Savior. He regularly asked others to pray for his father, and God answered their prayers. In 2006 Randy's father made a decision for Christ at an evangelistic crusade. The transformation was sudden and profound. Caring for his family replaced the carousing. Church attendance supplanted going to the bars. The power of the gospel improved the condition of their family and lit another lamp in the darkness.

People in Darkness

When Pastor Alberto Ledesma and the Quisqueya congregation first began talking about how they might minister more effectively in their part of Santo Domingo, they listed the many needs of their community. Their hearts were inevitably drawn to the children. As they looked around they saw street children with little stability. They found boys and girls trapped in a whirlpool of limited opportunity. The congregation decided it was time to do something about it.

The Quisqueya church began by initiating a children's program after school. In a short time they had 60 boys and girls gathering to learn Bible stories and receive English instruction. Soon their vision expanded. These faithful Nazarenes believed God had called them to be dynamic agents of transformation in their neighborhood, both spiritually and socially.

To help them more effectively minister to their community, the church leaders prepared a survey so they might gather data to corroborate what they had informally observed. Members of the congregation talked with more than 160 families in the blocks nearest the church building. In addition to taking a census of the number of children in the neighborhood, they asked questions about the make-up of the families, the number and ages of children in the home, educational experiences of both children and parents, and religious affiliation. They also inquired about interest in an enrichment program for kids in the neighborhood.

As the leaders looked at the results of the survey, they clearly saw the dire need around them. Their congregation was located in the midst of people who walked in darkness. They remembered that Jesus said, "I am the light of the world. Whoever follows me will never walk in darkness, but will have the light of life" (John 8:12). They remembered Jesus' charge to those who followed Him, "You are the light of the world" (Matt. 5:14*a*). And New Light Ministries was born.

New Light Ministries

The Quisqueya Church of the Nazarene launched New Light Ministries as a center for the holistic development of children. Through their programs they seek to provide training for children in a Christian environment. They also seek not only to equip the children, but transform families and their entire community through the grace and love of God.

New Light Ministries provides meals for
the children in the program.

Once they had the program ready, they invited prospective families to a dinner where they introduced New Light Ministries. They outlined the types of services the compassionate ministry center would provide the families. They described the registration requirements: the child must be from a family with limited income, must live in the neighborhood, and must not be receiving a scholarship from another school or training program. They intended to assist families not being served in any other way.

New Light Ministries provides instruction in four broad categories: educational, health and nutrition, social and emotional, and spiritual.

The educational program complements the instruction students receive at school. Every child in the program studies English and receives computer training—skills that will improve job prospects and help them prepare for higher education. Children also learn to play musical instruments. In the future they hope to offer teenagers training in cosmetology, dressmaking, woodworking, and computer repair.

Volunteers provide instruction in nutrition. Each child receives a healthy snack as part of the program, an important supplement for what sometimes is a subsistence diet. They discuss preventive healthcare and hygiene. Twice a year dental care is on the agenda with toothbrushes and toothpaste distributed to the children.

The staff constantly looks for ways to resolve the social and emotional distress of the children as well. They assess the children every six months with lesson plans written to address needs that arise. Topics such as honesty and the importance of healthy family interaction are examples of the type of subjects covered in the instruction.

Each age-group has devotions every time it meets. Bible study and prayer form an integral part of the New Light program. Children like Randy are encouraged to share their prayer requests, then rejoice when they see God's answers.

New Light Ministries began operating at a capacity of about 200 children and teens each week. They currently have seven groups that meet two or three times a week for two to three hours each session. Most days two

One of the classes in the New Light Ministries program

groups meet at the same time in different parts of the building. Originally the pastor lived in an apartment on the second floor of the church facility. The pastor moved to another house, and the congregation converted the parsonage into classrooms to accommodate the expanding ministry.

All parents of children in the New Light Ministries program meet once a month. The teachers review what the children are learning and provide additional information to the parents so that the lessons can be reinforced at home. They have plans for an increased adult education program, but that will have to wait until they are able to expand their facility.

churches in this part of Haiti provide
for their neighbors. The most ambitious
pleted in 1985 when Pastor Samerite
w that hand-dug a ditch for almost five
ed to lay a two-and-a-half-inch waterline
er from the source to where the people
structed three concrete cisterns to hold
result of this effort, 15,000 people have
drinking water. Wherever the Nazarenes
ells, the health of the people has improved
r of diseases has decreased. They are liter-
life in a cup of water.

ge Center

the people of the Ponce (Puerto Rico) First
the Nazarene looked at the 2000 census for
hborhood, they found that 74 percent of the
idents had income below the poverty line. Many
ople lived in that part of the city known as the
eighborhood of Ponce. Awareness of the need
a seed that blossomed into a compassionate min-
enter.

he congregation located an abandoned building
ne block from their church. In this historic district
ity maintains the exterior of a building in its original
l. The interior of this building, however, bore the
s of abuse. Drug users had gathered and built fires
ide. Once the church completed the purchase, the
anup began. Volunteers framed interior walls, painted,

Compassion Evangelism

In addition to his ministerial duties, Pastor Alberto also teaches the evangelism courses at the Dominican Republic Nazarene Bible College. He has implemented in his own congregation the methods he has taught to others. They have used the *JESUS* film. They have also formed home Bible studies to reach new people with the gospel. But the most effective evangelistic ministry has been the compassionate care of children and their families. New Light Ministries has become an integral part of the Quisqueya congregation.

Key leaders in New Light Ministries also serve the local congregation in various capacities. Rev. Lily Montaño de Ledesma functions as the director of the New Light Ministries program. She is the wife of Pastor Alberto and one of the persons discipled by Luis Daniel Perez (see chap. 5). Lily also serves as the copastor of the Quisqueya Church.

Dolores Florencio enrolled her two sons in the program. A short time later she began attending church services. By her own testimony she was a violent woman. Conflict with her husband made their home a dangerous place for the children. Two months after beginning to attend services at the Quisqueya Church, Dolores asked Jesus to forgive her sins. God answered her prayer. Dolores now works as the director of the nutrition program for New Light Ministries.

Angel Miguel Sosa felt insecure, empty, and depressed. He told lies to cover his destructive behavior.

Anxiety became unbearable. His marriage suffered, debts increased, and his children battled health problems. One day he heard a radio program about King David's prayer for God's mercy. At that moment Angel Miguel asked God to forgive him. That night, he said, he slept the most peacefully he had in a long time. A coworker invited Angel Miguel to go with him to the Quisqueya Church of the Nazarene. Immediately Angel Miguel felt at home. "That is my church," he said.

Angel Miguel now serves as the bookkeeper for the New Light Ministries. In addition, he teaches Sunday School and serves as the district NYI president. God called Angel Miguel to pastoral service in 2003, and he graduated from Bible college in January of 2007.

Average Sunday School attendance for the Quisqueya church was 37 in 2002. Largely because of the compassion evangelism through New Light Ministries, the average Sunday School attendance grew to 73 in 2006. Morning worship attendance jumped from 25 to 72 in just four years.

When the congregation launched the New Light Ministries, very few in the neighborhood knew much about the Quisqueya church. At first the congregation had a goal of building the church by reaching adults through children. God has been purifying their motives. They no longer consider children to be "hooks" by which to snag a few adults. The people who form the Quisqueya Church of the Nazarene now serve children compassionately simply because every person matters to Jesus. The Light has come and shines brightly in Santo Domingo.

A (

This they did, s

For Samerite Deruis
Southeast District, comp
life. He believes the discip
others in a holistic manner,
soul. Just as Jesus cared fo
leper and the lame, so the Je
loving attention to those who s
pelled by the love of God, even a
gospel (Mark 9:41).

Pastor Samerite has done
development as an expression of
than any other person in Haiti. Ofter
soon after planting a church on the
Nazarene schools now operate in the
erite also helped the community organi
ing project. The community planted trees
public land and even some private lar
export coffee to the United States, a great ec
fit to the people of this region.

Six Nazaren
community wells
project was cor
organized the c
miles. They nee
to carry the w
lived. They c
the water. As
access to fre
have put in
as the num
ally bringir

Golden

Wh
Church
their ne
4,745 re
older p
Sixth
plante
istry

just
the
for
sca
in
cl

The Golden Age Center in Ponce, Puerto Rico

and installed flooring. The Center now has approximately 2,700 square feet of space that includes a multipurpose room, a kitchen and dining room, an infirmary, and offices.

The doors of the Golden Age Center opened to receive new friends in March 2004. Residents of the neighborhood who are 60 years or older with limited income can apply for the program. As of the fall of 2006, over 30 people had enrolled with an additional 11 applications in process. The capacity is 50 senior adults. Except for one nurse, all of the staff volunteer their service. This includes a social worker, office staff, food service personnel, maintenance workers, the program director, etc.

The main activity room of the Golden Age Center

Open from 7:30 A.M. to 3:30 P.M. each weekday, the Golden Age Center provides a variety of services. Residents receive breakfast and lunch and are given a snack just before they leave in the afternoon. The participants enjoy a wide range of educational, cultural, and recreational activities. A nurse attends to health-care issues, and the Center provides transportation to doctors' appointments. Social and legal services are also available.

Financing for the Center comes from a variety of sources. The State of Puerto Rico provided a grant for operations. Individuals make donations. Most of the support, however, comes from the local congregation. The pastor voluntarily gave up part of her salary so the church could expand its compassionate ministry in the neighborhood. This relatively small congregation continues to serve Christ in a mighty way as they minister to their often marginalized neighbors.

Abandoned, but Not Forgotten

Compassionate ministry continues to be an integral expression of faith among Nazarenes in Cuba. Sometimes it is planned on the district level as "big brother" congregations assist people in need in "little brother" churches. Other times a local congregation will recognize a need and create ways to alleviate the distress.

For example, parents who remain behind when younger family members leave the country now have no family to care for them. But Jesus cares, and so do the Nazarenes.

They also care for children left with grandparents who are now too old to provide the necessary care. Institutions can do only so much, but Nazarenes show their love with regular visits.

Handicapped persons rarely see their family members. Nazarenes visit the 100 residents in one institution to play games and hold Sunday School classes.

Members of the Church of the Nazarene in one town went to the home of an elderly, sick man to care for him. Their expression of compassion deeply moved the man's daughter. She wanted to know more about the motivation for this selfless expression of love. The daughter has since invited church members to use her house for a prayer group.

Compassionate followers of Jesus will not leave anyone abandoned but will freely share the love and mercy so generously offered by God.

Hurricane Jeanne

When Hurricane Jeanne hit Haiti on September 19, 2004, the blow devastated the northern coastal city of Gonaïves. The storm displaced 80 percent of the city's 100,000 citizens due to horrific flooding. Some families clung to life by hanging in trees as the water swirled below. More than 3,000 died.

When the students at the Haiti Nazarene Bible College heard of the grim conditions in Gonaïves, they immediately decided to do what they could to help. Their initial plan was to take up a collection from among themselves. When others from outside the school heard of the effort, they asked to be involved too. People began bringing items to the campus. When they finally started north to Gonaïves, the students had 2,000 pounds of clothing and $1,000 (U.S.), a substantial sum for students who sometimes had difficulty making tuition payments.

Nazarene congregations in Gonaïves distributed the gifts to needy families. The winds of love blow strong in Haiti.

Educational Excellence Center

Across the street from the Church of the Nazarene in Cataño, Puerto Rico, a neglected city park provides cover for drug deals. This neighborhood, called Las

Vegas, has five public housing areas filled with families who face severe economic tension. Property crime statistics are high. A main employer in the town is a rum processing plant.

Many single-parent families live in Las Vegas. Since the mother has to work, her children often roam the streets after school. Few activities designed for children exist in the neighborhood. Few role models walk the streets. Even if they wanted to, parents often do not have sufficient education to adequately help their children excel. The one library in the area closed. No tutors are available. Many students drop out long before they graduate.

Gladybell grew up in Las Vegas. She married and moved to a nearby community. People often leave a place like Las Vegas for good, but not Gladybell. She knew firsthand the challenges children face in Las Vegas, so she drafted a proposal to start the Nazarene Family and Educational Excellence Center.

The purpose of the Center is clear and focused—to provide educational, social, and spiritual support for children and their families. They want to help kids succeed in school and reduce the number of dropouts in the community. They want to help families grow stronger and more resilient in the face of challenges.

Nazarene Compassionate Ministries provided $3,000 (U.S.) in startup funds. Individuals brought in school supplies and books. When the company that Gladybell's husband works for upgraded its computers, the company gave 30 old units to the Center.

The Center assists students in the first through ninth grades. In 2006 they averaged 30 students each day. Twenty students came from single-parent families; four students lived in foster homes. Twenty-five staff members volunteer at the Center, 10 volunteers each evening the Center is open. There is no need for an advertising campaign as parents pleased with the progress they see in their children tell other parents. Twenty students on a waiting list patiently hope additional volunteers will allow the program to expand.

> Child welfare workers removed Jesús from his home after his father stabbed him twice.

Using rooms in the church facility, the Center operates from 6:00 to 7:30 in the evening Monday through Thursday. They always begin with prayer then divide into groups by age and grade levels. Staff members help the students review lessons, complete homework, prepare for exams, and finish school projects.

Many people have witnessed the results of the Center. School teachers have written letters of commendation. Report cards have improved.

The father of a boy with Attention Deficit Disorder tried many schools without seeing improvement. The staff at the Center loved this young man and consistently helped as best they could. This boy has shown marked improvement since attending the Center.

In another situation, child welfare workers removed Jesús from his home after his father stabbed him twice in the head. A local school teacher suggested the foster mother take Jesús to the Center for additional assistance. Not only has this foster family found the Center a place for instruction, they discovered a church family as well.

Nazarenes in Cataño consider the Center to be in stage one of its development. In the future they would like to provide classes for adults as part of stage two. Computer training and English classes would help people get better jobs. They especially have a concern for equipping fathers. Stage three will be the establishment of a counseling center.

As followers of Jesus, Nazarenes in the Caribbean seek "to preach good news to the poor . . . to proclaim freedom for the prisoners and recovery of sight for the blind, to release the oppressed" (Luke 4:18). Whether it is offering a cup of water, befriending a lonely senior adult, or assisting a student who struggles to sit still in school, compassion reveals the goodness of the gospel and the grace of God.

Inspired 8ending

They . . . sent them off (Acts 13:3).

Three Work and Witness teams traveled to Point Fortin, Trinidad. The first team arrived from the North Florida District in 2000. The second and third teams arrived in Trinidad in 2003, the Maine District team in February and the Warwick Valley, New York, team in October.

Their mission was to work alongside the people of the Point Fortin Church of the Nazarene in the expansion of their church building. The sanctuary that had served the congregation for almost 40 years accommodated 120 people, but they averaged about 300 during Sunday morning worship services. The congregation desperately needed room to grow. They were surprised, however, when the largest growth came in the size of their hearts and their desire to serve others.

Once the Maine team became acclimated to the heat in Trinidad, a dramatic contrast to life at home in February, they went right to the task. The 19 members worked on the electrical system, poured a concrete walkway and stairs to the balcony, and painted the interior of the building. Each team member brought two suitcases: one with personal items and the second with things to give away, including clothing, bedding, food, and school supplies. The lasting impact of this trip, however, didn't originate with the construction project or the giving of gifts. Instead it came in the relationships that were formed. The night before the team returned home, people from the congregation came to the house where the team stayed. All seemed reluctant to leave.

The members of the Point Fortin church worked well alongside the team members. They were fascinated that people from the United States would give time, money, and effort to serve in the Caribbean. As they worked and pondered, some in the congregation began to see themselves as "going," not just "receiving." They started dreaming and planning to send a Work and Witness team to be a blessing to others just as they had been blessed.

Even before they completed their own project, the Point Fortin congregation began planning to send a team to Guyana in July 2002. One task force started raising money. Another collected used clothing. A third gathered food. The whole congregation became involved in the project, not just those who planned to make the trip. A prayer team blanketed the endeavor with intercession.

Thirty-three people made up this first Work and Witness team sent from the Point Fortin Church of the Nazarene. When they arrived in Guyana, they split into two work groups to complete projects at the La Grange and Sisters churches. They distributed 250 packages of food and clothing. Each evening the team led evangelistic services. The team from Point Fortin discovered the same thing the teams from the United States found to be true. The most important aspect of the trip was not the construction work or the dispersal of food and clothing, but the growing relationships with their Guyanese brothers and sisters.

When the team returned to Point Fortin, they felt like Paul and Barnabas returning to Antioch after the first missionary journey. The congregation rejoiced and praised God as the team reported on everything that God had done.

The reverberations through the Point Fortin congregation continued with increasing intensity. Maybe for the first time the congregation not only knew with their heads but also with their hearts that mission means "going."

They increased ministry in their community. Members started visiting patients in the hospital each week. Men in the congregation began to meet with those in prison. Others worked in a soup kitchen or delivered groceries to those in need.

The effect on the youth of the church may have been the most profound. Not only did the young members of the Work and Witness team learn about a different culture, their vision of the global church expanded. They discovered the joy of generosity and compassion. In response, the youth initiated a new ministry. Each month they organized a day when they visited the older members of their community and performed errands and chores.

Soon after the team returned from Guyana, they began planning a trip for 2003. Twenty-eight team members traveled to St. Vincent where they constructed bathrooms for the Rillan Hill church. They also held a weeklong Vacation Bible School for more than 100 children. In the evenings they participated in evangelistic services at the Arnos Vale Church of the Nazarene.

The next year the Point Fortin congregation sent 28 team members to Suriname. They spent the first night at the District Center in Guyana. Three Guyanese joined them for the 16-hour bus ride to the work site. The team painted the building for a Haitian Creole congregation and built a fence and toilet facilities. They also built a fence for a Dutch congregation. When they returned to the District Center in Guyana, team members noted the work that needed to be done there. So they purchased a new office chair, painted the office, and refinished bookcases and a desk. They worked until 2:30 in the morning and left for the airport 90 minutes later.

In 2005 the Point Fortin congregation selected Antigua as the destination for their Work and Witness team. The 20 team members assisted with the construction of the Living Water Church of the Nazarene. They worked from 6:30 in the morning to 6:00 in the evening with only an afternoon break at one of the 365 beaches in Antigua. Team members also conducted a Vacation Bible School for about 200 children. In the evenings they held evangelistic services.

Other places in the Caribbean began organizing mission teams as well. Twenty-six people from the Blades

Two girls from Antigua

Hill church in Barbados traveled to Dominica in 2004. The first week they conducted a Vacation Bible School. The second week they participated in evangelistic outreach with the Gaulette River congregation.

In April 2005 the Leeward/Virgin Islands District sent a team to Grenada where Hurricane Ivan had wrecked the Fontenoy church. The 25 team members, including 11 youth, fixed the roof, replaced glass in windows, repaired the electrical system, replaced fixtures, and painted the building inside and out. They also constructed an apartment for the pastor with a living room, kitchen, and bedroom.

The San Fernando church in Trinidad reported 136 members in 2006. This congregation sent a team to Guyana in July of that year to work on construction projects for several congregations. They led evangelistic services in three locations each night, including one in an area where they were planting a church. The team also provided two gospel concerts during the trip.

Three Work and Witness teams from the United States thought they were merely helping a growing congregation expand their church building. They did much more than that—they inspired the people of Point Fortin "toward love and good deeds" (Heb. 10:24). Others caught the vision. Nazarenes in the Caribbean eagerly go to serve others in the name of Jesus.

Basic Training Camp

Twenty-four teenagers from the United States arrived at the Dominican Republic Oriental District campground after dark on June 28, 2004. Teenagers from the Dominican Republic and Puerto Rico awaited them. The electricity had gone out, and the backup generator wouldn't operate, so introductions were made in the shadows. The spark ignited that first night, however, soon glowed brightly.

These teenagers from three countries had one important thing in common: they believed God had called them to be missionaries. The Basic Training Camp provided an opportunity for them to explore the life of a missionary and learn about ministry in a cross-cultural

Poster from the Basic Training Camp held in the Dominican Republic in 2004

setting. All sessions were presented in both English and Spanish.

The organizers wanted the students to experience a variety of missionary tasks. Evangelism was the theme for one day. After classroom instruction, the teens traveled through a village inviting people to a *JESUS* film showing. In all, 614 people responded to the invitation and attended the film that night. Courtney, one of the teens from the United States, smiled as the Dominicans applauded every time Jesus performed a miracle. She felt that evening was paramount in the whole cross-cultural experience. After watching the film, 14 people made a decision for Christ and 23 others requested someone visit them for Bible study.

To learn about Work and Witness, the teens painted restrooms and built an outdoor barbecue grill at the campground where they were staying. Another day was given to compassionate ministries. They distributed vitamins and personal care products. They also enjoyed many other learning activities, such as leading a Vacation Bible School and attending worship services.

For Courtney, this trip to the Caribbean for the Basic Training Camp confirmed her own call to missionary service. She appreciated the opportunity to become acquainted with other young people who had a similar vision for ministry. For Christie, also from the United States, "life-changing" is a phrase that falls short of adequately describing what happened to her while attending the camp. She felt her life's "glasses" had been cleaned as she saw the world from a new perspective. Dhariana, from the Dominican Republic, rejoiced at what happened that week. "It was amazing to see how we, from different cultures, colors, and languages became one body in Jesus, praying, worshiping, talking, eating, and serving others together."

Missionary Preparation in the Caribbean

In the mid-1960s, college students from the United States expressed a growing interest in a summer mission program, something that had never been tried before. Denominational leaders weighed the risks and rewards before working out the details of a program that was to become known as Student Mission Corps. Appropriate boards gave the approval in January 1967, and the first 16 student missionaries were deployed in June.

At the beginning, leaders wanted to keep the students as close to the United States as possible. They also decided that English-speaking countries would provide the quickest start for the students. Naturally, they looked to the Caribbean as the location in which to launch this new endeavor. After three days of training and orientation in Kansas City, the students left for Barbados, British Honduras (now Belize), Guyana, Puerto Rico, and Trinidad. After a successful first year, 29 students participated in Student Mission Corps in 1968.

Youth in Mission is the name of the current Nazarene summer program for college students. In 2005 the first international Youth in Mission team was organized with a representative from every region in the Church of the Nazarene. Members of the team came from the Dominican Republic, Guatemala, Hungary, Peru, South Africa, South Korea, and the United States.

This international team began with two weeks of service in Kansas City. They worked at the Kansas City Urban Youth Center, an inner-city ministry; True Light Church of the Nazarene, an urban congregation; and

> In 2005 the first international Youth in Mission team was organized with a representative from every region in the Church of the Nazarene.

Central Church of the Nazarene in a suburban setting where they assisted with Vacation Bible School. Then they traveled to Indianapolis where they participated in the One Heart Many Hands outreach project prior to the 2005 General Assembly and Conventions.

Just the previous year Dhariana had participated in Basic Training Camp, but in 2005 she represented the Caribbean on this international Youth in Mission team. These experiences provided further confirmation that God had called her to be a missionary. Following the summer with Youth in Mission, Dhariana's involvement in the Caribbean Region increased. She served as secretary in the Spanish field office. As the child development coordinator for Nazarene Compassionate Ministry (NCM) in the Caribbean, Dhariana supervised several projects and worked closely with the various field coordinators. She also provided translations between Spanish and English as needed and coordinated regional activities with the NCM office in Kansas City. For the 2005-2009 quadrennium, Dhariana served as the Spanish field representative to the regional NYI Council. In this role she acted as the liaison between local churches and regional leaders and assisted with leadership training and resource development.

Beginning in October 2007, Dhariana began serving as a volunteer missionary for the Church of the Nazarene. Church leaders met in Monterrey, Mexico, in May of 2006 to discuss how districts and congregations in northern Mexico and the southern United States might collaborate to promote growth in existing churches and to plant new ministries. Dhariana, a young woman from the Caribbean, moved to El Paso, Texas, as a missionary with the Border Initiative.

Island Legacy

On Paul's second missionary journey he met a young man named Timothy. The members of the church in that region spoke well of this young believer. As a result, Paul invited Timothy to join his missionary endeavor. Under Paul's tutelage, Timothy matured as a minister of the gospel of Jesus Christ. We are reminded of his example as a pastor when excerpts of Paul's letter to Timothy are read at ordination services.

The Caribbean Region has played a key role in the training of young missionaries. The cycle has come full circle. Because of its proximity to the United States, the Caribbean has been a convenient locale for young people to gain cross-cultural ministry experience. Now the Church of the Nazarene is training teenagers from various cultures and countries together. Youth in the Caribbean, like Dhariana, are answering God's call and preparing for a life of service to God and the church. These young people are ready to go in the name of Christ to any place where their service is needed. And the missionary fervor of the Church of the Nazarene continues on to the next generation.

Praise God in the Islands

News spread quickly when Paul and Barnabas returned to Antioch after their first missionary journey. The congregation gathered to hear the stories of how God had used the missionaries they had sent (Acts 14:26-28). Paul told them about ministry in the synagogues until the leaders became jealous of the large number of those attracted to the gospel. He also told them about the eager reception among the Gentiles. And he described the churches that had been planted and the leaders appointed to oversee the congregations.

The people rejoiced at what they heard. They now had firm evidence that following the Holy Spirit's direction resulted in the spread of the gospel.

In the same way, we rejoice in what God is doing in the Caribbean among the believers called Nazarenes. People throughout the region hear the good news that Jesus is the Savior. Believers send the roots of their faith down deep as they learn more about living in the way of Jesus. When the Christ-followers in the Caribbean learn of a need, they find compassionate ways to meet it as an

Flowers along the beach on St. Martin

expression of their love for God. And when God calls, they respond, "Here am I. Send me!" (Isa. 6:8*b*).

> *Sing to the L*ORD *a new song,*
> *his praise from the ends of the earth,*
> *you who go down to the sea, and all that is in it,*
> *you islands, and all who live in them.*
> *Let them give glory to the L*ORD
> *and proclaim his praise in the islands (Isa. 42:10, 12).*

Afterword

The Four Fields of the Caribbean Region

Spanish Field
Cuba (begun in 1902)
Puerto Rico (1944)
Dominican Republic (1974)

English Field
Barbados (1926)
Trinidad and Tobago (1926)
Belize (1934)
St. Croix (1944)
Guyana (1946)
Jamaica (1966)
Bahamas (1971)
St. Lucia (1972)
Antigua (1973)
Dominica (1974)
St. Vincent (1975)
Grenada (1977)
St. Kitts-Nevis (1983)

French Field
Haiti (1950)
Martinique (1976)
Guadeloupe (1986)

French Guiana (1988)
St. Martin (1994)

Dutch Field
Suriname (1984)
Aruba (2000)

For a brief history of the work of the Church of the Nazarene in each country, please go to www.caribnaz.org, then to the "Countries" drop down menu.

Call to Action

After reading this book, please consider doing one or more of the following:

1. Go to www.caribnaz.org to read a recent issue of *Caribbean Tides,* the official publication of the region. You'll find stories and photos of ministry in the Caribbean. *Caribbean Tides* is published in English, French, and Spanish.
2. While you're at this web site, provide your E-mail address in order to receive the E-newsletter from the Caribbean regional office.
3. Consider forming a Work and Witness team to do a project in the Caribbean. Go to www.caribnaz.org, then to the "W&W" drop down menu to see available projects.
4. Contact the JESUS Film Harvest Partners office about the possibility of a *JESUS* Film Ministry Trip to the Caribbean. For more information, go to www.jfhp.org, then to the "Get Involved" drop down menu. Or call (913) 663-5700.
5. Pastor Prayer Cards are available at www.caribnaz.org. Go to the "Quick Links" drop down menu, choose "Pastor Prayer Cards," then click on the name of a country. Photos of pastors mentioned in this book can be found there.

Pronunciation Guide

Chapter 1
Carlos Moises	CAHR-lohs MOY-ses
Cayes	KIE
Guyana	gie-A-nah
Guiana	gee-AH-nah
Leontis Augustin	lay-OHN-tees ou-GOOS-teen
Papiamento	PAH-pee-ah-MEN-toh
St. Croix	SAYNT KROY
Suriname	ser-uh-NAHM-uh

Chapter 2
Barrio	BAH-ree-oh
Ceiba	SAY-bah
Gilma Madera	GIL-mah mah-DE-rah
Guanabo	gwah-NAH-boh
Holguín	ahl-GEEN
Idalmis Fernandez	ee-DAHL-mees fer-NAN-dez
Julio	HEW-lee-oh

Chapter 3
Cayenne	kie-EN
Chanka	CHAHN-kah
Guadeloupe	gwah-duh-LOOP-ay
Kennet	KEN-net
Mandeville	MAHN-day-vil
Marigot	MAR-ree-goh
Orjala	ohr-YAH-lah
Porus	POH-ruhs
Taki-Taki	TAH-kee TAH-kee

Chapter 4

Andrèenne Pavilus	ahn-DRAY-en PAH-vah-luhs
Cité Soleil	see-TAY soh-LAY
Destinè	des-tee-NAY
Louis Marie Lourde	loo-EES mah-REE LOORD
Sadrack	SAD-rak

Chapter 5

Pueblo Viejo	PWE-bloh vee-AY-hoh

Chapter 6

Angel Miguel Sosa	ahn-HEL mee-GEL SOH-sah
Florencio	floh-REN-see-yoh
Ledesma	lay-DAYS-mah
Montaño de Ledesma	mawn-TAWN-yoh day lay-DAYS-mah
Quisqueya	kees-KAY-ah

Chapter 7

Cataño	kah-TAHN-yoh
Gonaïves	GOA-nie-eev
Ponce	PAWN-say
Samerite Deruisseau	sah-MER-ee-tay de-REW-soh

Chapter 8

Dhariana	dah-ree-AH-nah
Fontenoy	FAHN-ten-oy
Fortin	FOHR-tin
Gaulette	gah-YET
Grenada	gre-NA-duh
La Grange	lah GRAYNJ
Rillan	ree-LAHN